LET'S LEARN ABOUT COMPUTER SCIENCE

PROGRAMMING

Jeff Mapua

Enslow Publishing
101 W. 23rd Street
Suite 240
New York, NY 10011
USA
enslow.com

WORDS TO KNOW

algorithm A step-by-step way to solve a problem.

application A computer program.

browser A computer program that lets you explore the internet.

code Instructions for a computer in a language it understands.

data Information that is used in a computer.

language A set of signs, symbols, and rules. They are used to give directions to a computer.

program Step-by-step instructions that tell a computer what to do with data.

programmer A person who writes computer programs.

syntax The rules for a language.

task A job.

CONTENTS

A programmer works at a computer.

Using Computers

Have you ever used a computer? A computer by itself is just a machine. It must wait to be told what to do. A **programmer** is a person who writes instructions that tell a computer what to do.

FAST FACT

The first computer programmer was a woman named Ada Lovelace.

We use instructions when we put something together. A computer program is a set of instructions.

Programs

A programmer writes **programs**.
A program is a set of step-by-step instructions. They tell a computer what to do with **data**.

FAST FACT

People write programs that can harm your computer or steal your data. They are called malware.

An algorithm is like a recipe. They both explain how to do something in steps.

What Programs Do

A program's instructions are like a recipe. They tell a computer what to do one step at a time. Programs tell a computer what to do and how to do it. **Algorithms** tell the computer how to do a **task**.

FAST FACT

In 2009, a computer programmer released the game Minecraft. It was later sold for $2.5 billion.

A computer program allows you to surf the internet.

Types of Programs

Programs can be anything a computer does. You use a program called a web **browser** to surf the internet. Programs are sometimes called **applications**, or apps.

FAST FACT

Some programmers write programs to protect people from the harmful ones.

It is hard to ask for directions if you do not speak the same language! Computers do not understand the same words that you do.

Speaking Computer

A computer does not understand words like people do. It only understands special **languages**. A programmer must learn a special language. Then the programmer can tell a computer what to do.

FAST FACT

Many websites use more than one language. They include HTML, CSS, and Javascript.

Some people understand sign language. Computers understand their own special languages.

Languages

Computers understand many languages. Popular languages include Java, C++, Python, and Ruby. Programs can be written in one of these languages.

FAST FACT

There have been around 700 computer languages used so far.

Rules are important. You follow rules in class. Computer languages follow their own rules.

Syntax

The English language has its own rules. You follow the rules when you read and speak. Computer languages have their own rules. These rules are called **syntax**.

This child is coding on his computer.

Editor

An editor is a kind of computer program. It helps programmers write in a computer language. What a programmer writes is called computer **code**.

FAST FACT

Today's cell phones have more code than space shuttles did in the 1970s.

Your car uses code! It has its own computer that helps it run.

Uses for Coding

Coding is used for many things. Applications and games on smartphones and computers are coded. Websites are also built with code.

FAST FACT

Some streetlights, tires, bikes, and shoes use computer code.

Activity

Fun with Programming

MATERIALS
notebook
pencil

Want to learn more about programming? Here are some ideas: Make up a secret code. Think of a way to change the letters of your name into different letters, numbers, or symbols. Come up with different letters, numbers, or symbols for the rest of the alphabet. Then write a sentence using your secret code.

Write "code" to tell a machine how to make a sandwich. Decide on what kind of sandwich you want. Make step-by-step instructions for an imaginary machine to make a sandwich starting with getting bread. Then write instructions for getting other ingredients.

Learn More

Books

Anniss, Matt. *Understanding Programming & Logic*. London: Raintree, 2016.

Bedell, J. M. *So, You Want to Be a Coder?: The Ultimate Guide to a Career in Programming, Video Game Creation, Robotics, and More!* New York, NY: Aladdin, 2016.

Wainewright, Max. *How to Code*. New York, NY: Sterling, 2016.

Websites

Made w/ Code
www.madewithcode.com
Find fun coding projects to help get started in the world of programming.

Scratch
scratch.mit.edu
Visit Scratch and program your own stories and games!

Index

Published in 2019 by Enslow Publishing, LLC.
101 W. 23rd Street, Suite 240, New York, NY 10011

Library of Congress Cataloging-in-Publication Data

Names: Mapua, Jeff, author.
Title: Programming / Jeff Mapua.
Description: New York, NY : Enslow Publishing, 2019. | Series: Let's learn about computer science | Includes bibliographical references and index. |
Audience: Grades K to 4.
Identifiers: LCCN 2018005416| ISBN 9781978501799 (library bound) | ISBN 9781978502314 (pbk.) | ISBN 9781978502321 (6 pack)
Subjects: LCSH: Computer programming—Juvenile literature.
Classification: LCC QA76.6115 .M37 2019 | DDC 005.1—dc23

LC record available at https://lccn.loc.gov/2018005416

Printed in the United States of America

To Our Readers: We have done our best to make sure all website addresses in this book were active and appropriate when we went to press. However, the author and the publisher have no control over and assume no liability for the material available on those websites or on any websites they may link to. Any comments or suggestions can be sent by email to customerservice@enslow.com.

Photos Credits: Cover, p. 1 Ollyy/Shutterstock.com; pp. 2, 3, 24 Best-Backgrounds/Shutterstock.com; p. 4 nd3000/Shutterstock.com; p. 6 VGstockstudio/Shutterstock.com; p. 8 Impact Photography/Alamy Stock Photo; p. 10 Andrey_Popov/Shutterstock.com; p. 12 Iakov Filimonov/Shutterstock.com; p. 14 Monika Wisniewska/Shutterstock.com; p. 16 Maskot/Getty Images; p. 18 Phil's Mommy/Shutterstock.com; p. 20 Kzenon/Shutterstock.com; p. 23 Pressmaster/Shutterstock.com; interior design elements (laptop) ArthurStock/Shutterstock.com, (flat screen computer) Aleksandrs Bondars/Shutterstock.com.